Family and Friends 3

Sinbad

By Janet Hardy-Gould
Illustrated by Dave Neale

OXFORD
UNIVERSITY PRESS

Before you read ...

1 This is Sinbad. Where does he come from? Circle.

a Athens

b Baghdad

c Istanbul

d Cairo

2 Sinbad has many adventures. Match the words with the pictures.

1 ship

2 sea monster

3 storm

4 island

5 captain

6 raft

7 whale

8 jewels

a 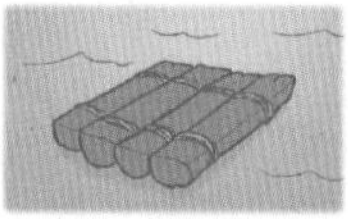

b 

c 

d 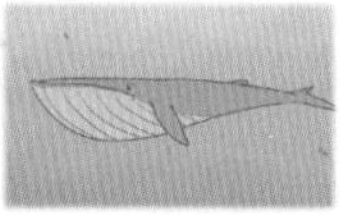

e 

f 

g 

h 

OUR story begins in old Baghdad. A rich old man is very ill in bed. He calls to his son, Sinbad.
'I'm dying, Sinbad,' says the old man. 'You can have all my money, my son. But you must be careful with it.'
'Please don't die, Father,' says Sinbad.

ill

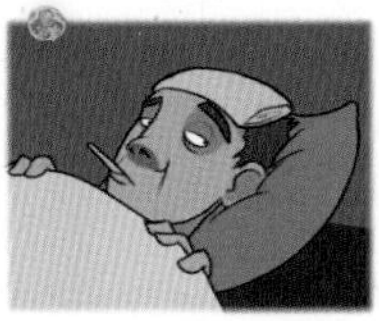

money

rich

Sinbad's father dies and Sinbad is unhappy for a long time. But one day he thinks, 'I'm a very lucky man. I have got a lot of money now, some beautiful things and a big house.'

Sinbad buys new things to wear and expensive things to eat with his father's money. Every evening Sinbad's friends come to his house. They have a big dinner and laugh all night.

expensive

laugh

lucky

unhappy

But after a year, Sinbad has got no more money. 'What can I do?' he thinks. He looks at the things in his father's house. He sees all the beautiful carpets. Suddenly he has an idea.

'I can sail to different countries,' Sinbad thinks. 'And I can sell these carpets for a lot of money.'

Sinbad finds an old ship with a very old captain. Three days later, Sinbad is ready to leave Baghdad. He talks to all the men on the ship. 'I want to sell my carpets and bring back a lot of money,' he tells them.

captain

carpet

sell

ship

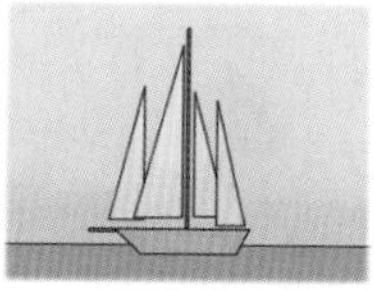

The ship sails away from Baghdad and out to sea. After ten days at sea, Sinbad is very thirsty. He sees a beautiful island. 'Please stop!' he says to the captain. Sinbad and some of the sailors go onto the island. Sinbad takes a barrel. He wants to look for some water.

barrel

island

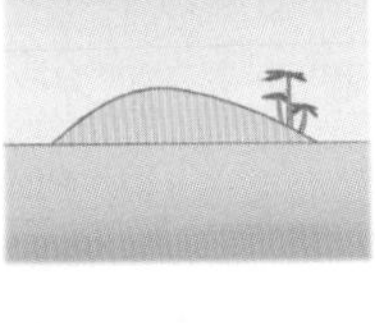

sailor

sea

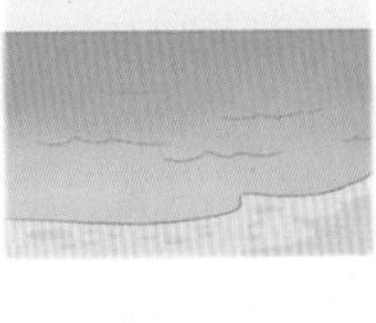

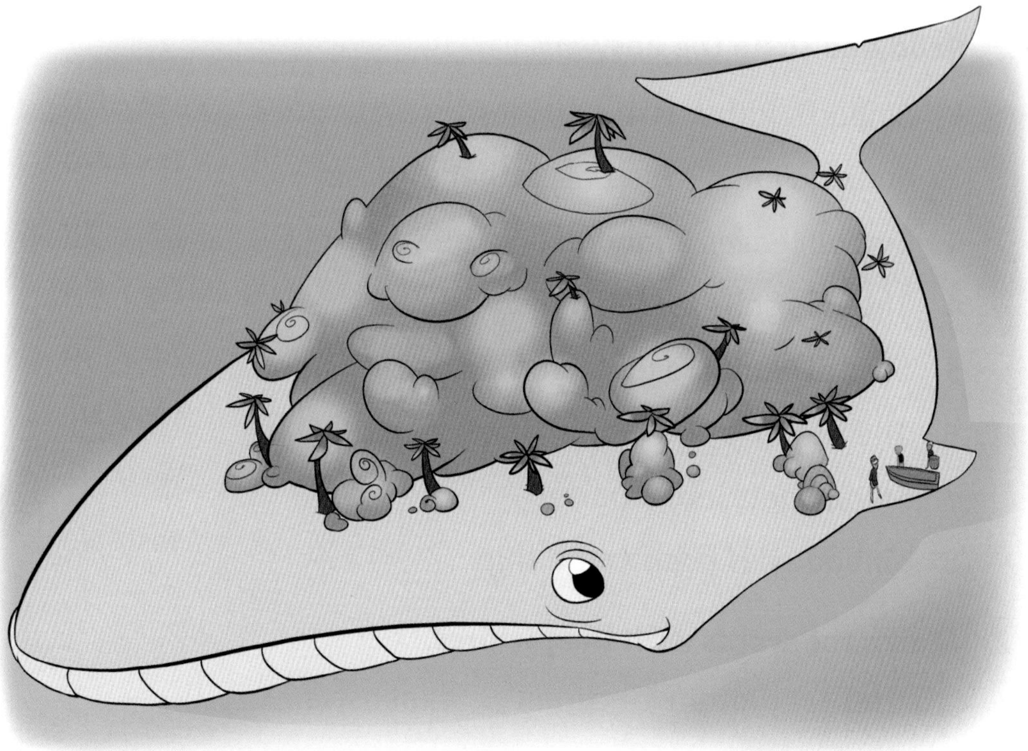

'What a wonderful island!' says Sinbad. They begin to look for water. But suddenly the island moves.
'The island is moving!' says Sinbad.
'Oh no!' cry the sailors. 'This isn't an island. It's a whale!'
The whale moves down into the water. All the sailors are in the sea.
'Help! Help!' they cry.
Sinbad quickly gets into the barrel.
Now he is at sea in the barrel.
'Hello! Hello!' he cries again and again. But nobody answers.

move

whale

1 Read and circle the answers.

1 Sinbad's father is ill and dies. Yes / No
2 Sinbad wants to sell his father's house. Yes / No
3 Sinbad leaves Baghdad on a new ship. Yes / No
4 The ship sails for ten days. Yes / No
5 Sinbad wants to look for food on the island. Yes / No
6 The island is a whale. Yes / No
7 Sinbad gets into a barrel. Yes / No
8 Sinbad goes back to the ship. Yes / No

2 Match the words with the pictures.

barrel | captain | carpet | expensive | ill | ~~island~~ | money | ship

1 island

2 ______

3 ______

4 ______

5 ______

6 ______

7 ______

8 ______

3 Read and match.

1 Sinbad lives — a with his friends.
2 Sinbad's father was — b in a barrel.
3 Sinbad has dinner — c down into the sea.
4 Sinbad is going to — d a rich man.
5 Sinbad sees — e in Baghdad.
6 The whale moves — f a beautiful island.
7 Sinbad is at sea — g sell his father's carpets.

4 What happens next? Choose.

a ☐ Sinbad finds the ship again.

b ☐ Sinbad comes to a small island.

c ☐ Sinbad sells his carpets and gets lots of money.

Sinbad's barrel moves on the sea all night. In the morning he looks out and sees a small island. Soon the barrel comes to the island and Sinbad gets out.
Suddenly the sky becomes black. Sinbad feels afraid.
'Help! What's happening?' he cries. He looks up at the sky.
A very big bird is flying nearer and nearer.
'Oh, no!' he thinks, 'That bird is a Roc.'

bird

sky

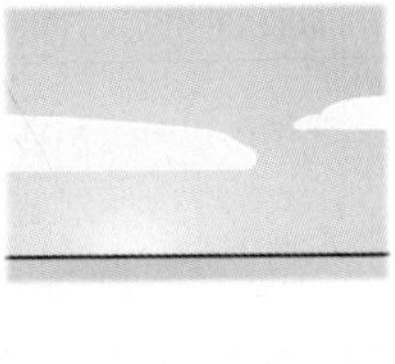

The Roc sits down and goes to sleep. Sinbad takes off his turban and he puts it around the Roc's leg. 'When the Roc flies away, I can leave the island, too,' he thinks. After some time, the Roc wakes up and flies away. Sinbad flies up into the sky with the bird. The Roc flies for hours and hours. In the end it flies down into a valley and lands there.

land	sleep	turban	valley
			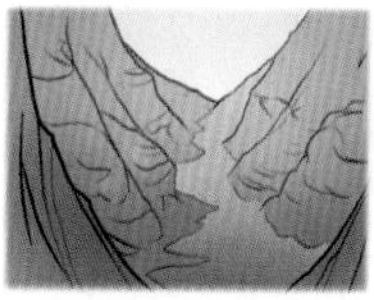

In the valley Sinbad finds lots of little rocks. 'What are these?' he thinks. 'I know!' he cries. 'They're jewels!' And he puts some of them in his bag.

Then he hears a noise. There are three big snakes behind him.

He runs away very fast. In front of him he sees a dead animal.

He goes behind the animal and waits. Soon a Roc flies down and takes the dead animal up into the sky. Quickly Sinbad puts his arms around the dead animal. He flies up into the sky with the Roc.

animal

dead

jewels

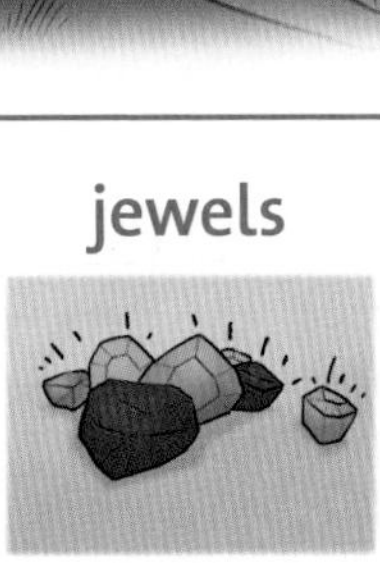

rock

The Roc flies out of the valley and it lands near a village. The men from the village run to see it, then the Roc flies away. Sinbad comes out from under the dead animal.
'Who are you?' ask the men from the village.
'I'm Sinbad the Sailor,' he says. 'I was in the valley.'
The people are surprised. 'Nobody goes into the valley,' they say. 'The snakes eat everything there.'
'Not me!' laughs Sinbad.
'You're very lucky!' they say.
Sinbad wants to go back to Baghdad. He gives the jewels to the people and they find a ship for him. When Sinbad arrives in Baghdad he meets his friends.
'Is it you, our old friend Sinbad?' they ask.
'Yes. But I'm Sinbad the Sailor now!' he says. And he tells them about his adventures.

adventure

surprised

1 Complete the sentences.

1 On the island, Sinbad looks up and sees a big ...

a ☐ snake. b ☐ whale. c ☑ bird.

2 Sinbad flies with the Roc and lands ...

a ☐ on the ship. b ☐ in a valley. c ☐ in Baghdad.

3 In the valley Sinbad finds lots of ...

a ☐ carpets. b ☐ jewels. c ☐ money.

4 Sinbad runs away from ...

a ☐ a dead animal. b ☐ a Roc. c ☐ snakes.

5 The people in the village think that Sinbad is ...

a ☐ lucky. b ☐ ill. c ☐ rich.

2 Look at the pictures and write the words.

1 t u r b a n

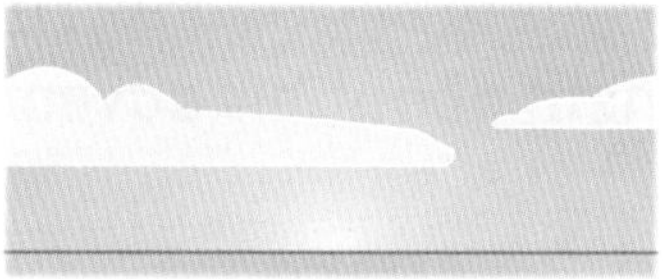

2 s __ __

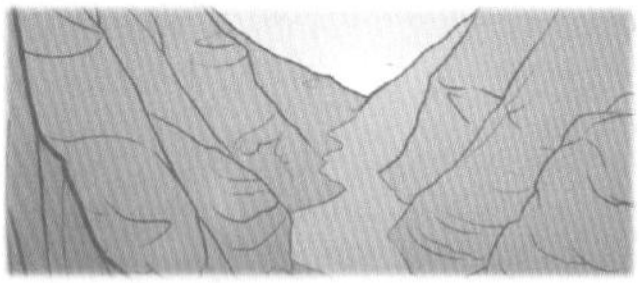

3 v __ __ __ __ __

4 a __ __ __ __ __

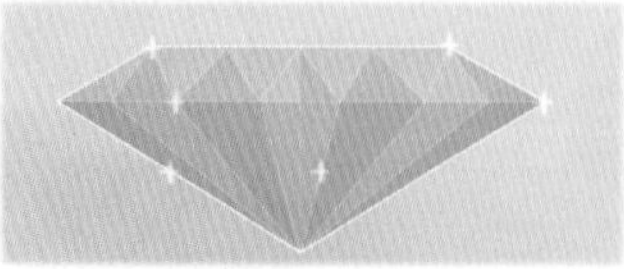

5 j __ __ __ __

6 a __ v __ __ __ __ __ __

3 Order the words.

1 arrives | on | an island | Sinbad | .

Sinbad arrives on an island.

____

2 bird | in the sky | . | is | A big | flying

____

3 . | flies | the Roc | Sinbad | with | into the sky

____

4 some jewels | puts | into | . | his bag | He

____

5 three | Sinbad | . | behind | big snakes | There are

____

6 in Baghdad | . | his friends | Sinbad | meets

____

4 What happens next? Choose.

a ☐ Sinbad stays in Baghdad.

b ☐ Sinbad sails away again.

c ☐ A Roc wants to eat Sinbad.

Sinbad's friends come to visit him at his father's house. But there is nothing to eat or drink, and there are no carpets in the house. His friends soon go away.

'I need some more adventures,' thinks Sinbad.

The next morning Sinbad finds a ship and a captain, and soon he's ready to leave Baghdad again.

After a week at sea, the ship arrives at an island.

'That's the island of Zugab,' says the captain.

Sinbad gets off the boat and explores the island with two of the sailors.
Suddenly the sky goes black and there's a big storm.
The storm takes the ship far out to sea. Sinbad and the two sailors are now the only people on the island. They climb behind some big rocks and when night comes they go to sleep. In the morning they find a very big snake around them. The snake eats one of the sailors.

climb

explore

storm

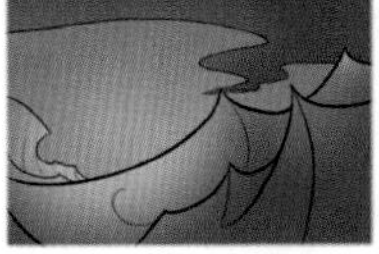

Quickly Sinbad and the second sailor climb a tree. They stay there all day and all night. When Sinbad wakes up in the morning, he's alone.
'Oh no! The second sailor is dead, too,' he thinks. 'And I'm the snake's next breakfast!'
Just then Sinbad sees some wood near the tree. He climbs down the tree and he makes some armour from the wood, then he climbs the tree again. Sinbad stays in his armour all night. The snake moves around him, but it can't eat Sinbad.

alone

armour

tree

wood

In the morning Sinbad sees a ship out at sea. 'I know that ship,' he thinks. 'It's my old ship!'

The snake is sleeping in the sun near the tree. Sinbad quietly climbs down the tree. Then he runs to the sea. The snake wakes up and comes after him. But Sinbad runs faster and gets to the sea before the snake can eat him. Sinbad swims to the ship.

'It's Sinbad!' cry the sailors. 'You're a very lucky man! We have all your beautiful carpets from Baghdad!'

'Thank you!' says Sinbad.

The ship sails home. It stops at lots of different countries and Sinbad sells all his carpets. When he arrives in Baghdad he has got a lot of money.

---

sail

wake up

1 Complete the sentences.

1 Sinbad leaves Baghdad because he wants ...
a ☑ more adventures. b ☐ more jewels.

2 Sinbad explores the island of Zugab with ...
a ☐ some sailors. b ☐ the captain.

3 On the island of Zugab the snake eats ...
a ☐ one sailor. b ☐ two sailors.

4 Sinbad finds some wood and makes ...
a ☐ some armour. b ☐ a barrel.

5 Sinbad goes back to Baghdad with ...
a ☐ a lot of carpets. b ☐ a lot of money.

2 Look at the pictures and write the words.

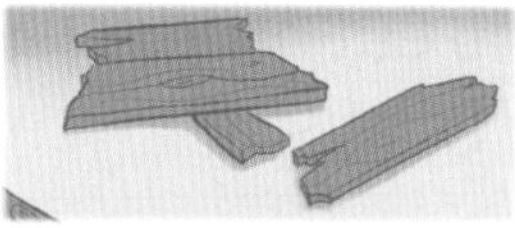

1 o d o w wood

2 r o m a r u ____________

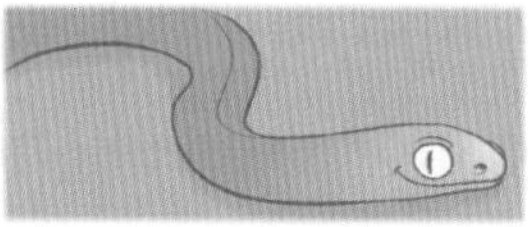

3 k e s a n ____________

4 m o t r s ____________

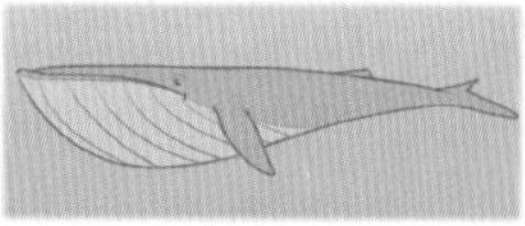

5 l e w a h ____________

6 l o s i r a ____________

3 Complete the story with the words.

arrives | climbs | explores | ~~leaves~~

makes | runs | swims | wakes up

Sinbad [1] ___leaves___ Baghdad. After a week the ship [2] ____________ at the island of Zugab. Sinbad [3] ____________ the island. He finds a very big snake! Sinbad [4] ____________ some armour and [5] ____________ a tree. In the morning he sees a ship and he [6] ____________ to the sea. The snake [7] ____________ and comes after him but Sinbad is faster. Sinbad [8] ____________ to the ship.

4 What happens next? Choose.

a ☐ Sinbad stays at home and writes about his adventures.

b ☐ Sinbad goes to sea again for more adventures.

c ☐ Sinbad goes back to the island of Zugab and finds lots of jewels.

Sinbad meets his friends and he tells them all about his adventures. But after some time Sinbad is not happy in Baghdad.

'I want to go back to sea,' he tells his friends.

A week later Sinbad leaves Baghdad on a big, tall ship. He's very excited.

'It's time for some more adventures,' he tells the captain.

The ship sails for three weeks. But one night there's a storm, the ship breaks here and there, and it must land. In the morning the ship arrives in a new country.

break

country

excited

Sinbad sees some people. They take Sinbad to their king. Sinbad tells the king about his wonderful adventures. The king listens carefully.
'You're a lucky man,' he says. 'You can make us lucky, too. You must marry my daughter.'
When Sinbad sees her beautiful face, he falls in love with her at once.
Sinbad marries the king's daughter in front of the king and all the people.

fall in love

marry

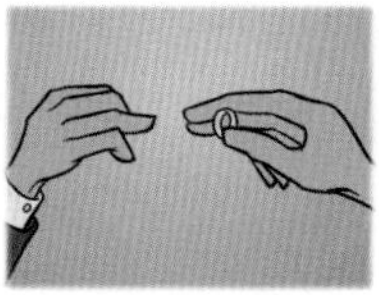

A year after the wedding, the king's daughter becomes ill. A friend talks to Sinbad quietly.
'Be careful! When a woman dies in this country, they bury the husband with her,' he says.
'What?' cries Sinbad.
The king's daughter becomes very ill, and in the end she dies. The king buries Sinbad with his daughter. He also buries lots of jewels with them. Sinbad is now far under the ground. He closes his eyes and he waits to die. But suddenly he sees an animal near him. It's a big, strange, black and white animal. Sinbad puts lots of jewels in his bag and he quickly follows the animal through the ground.

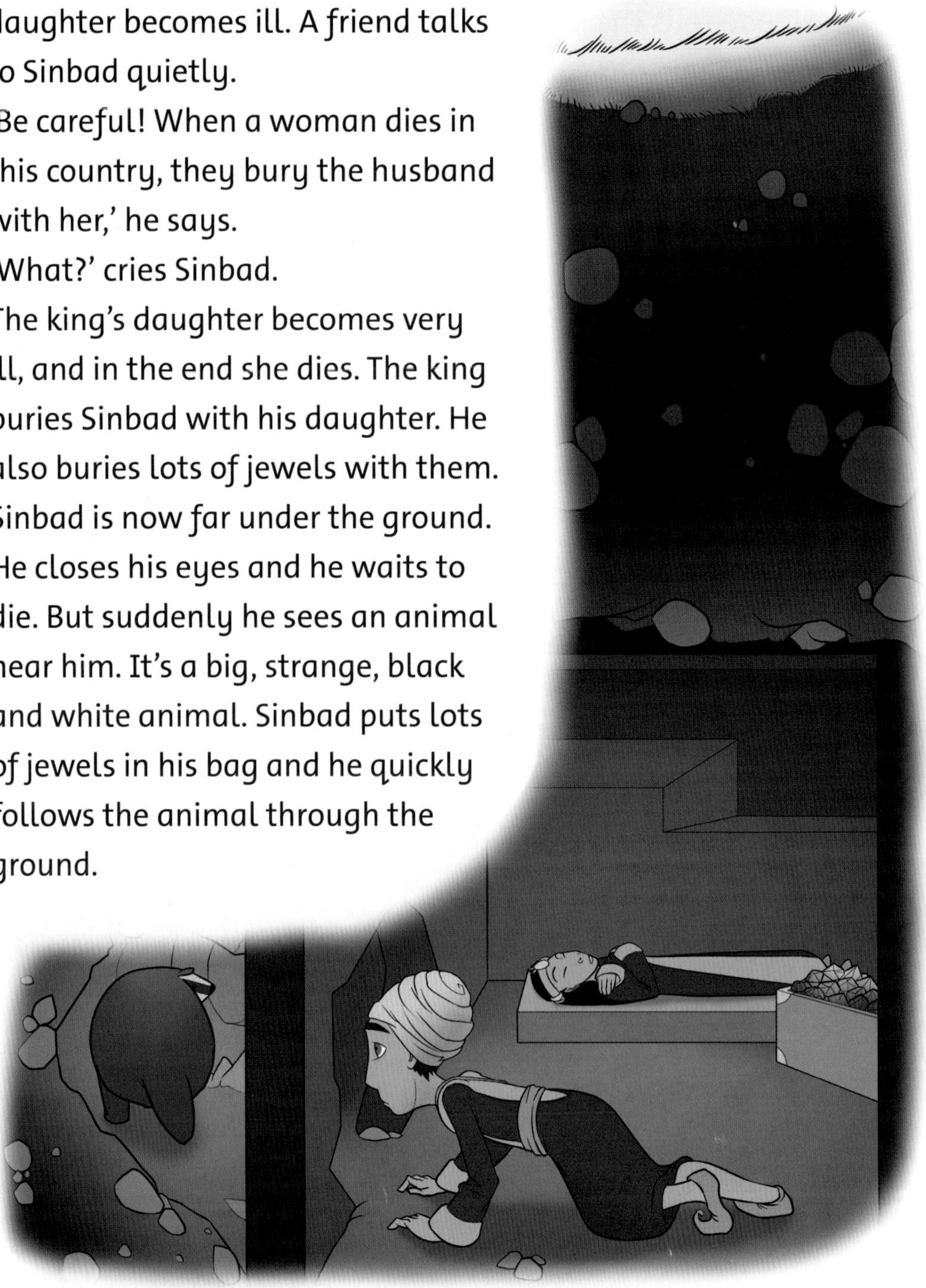

bury

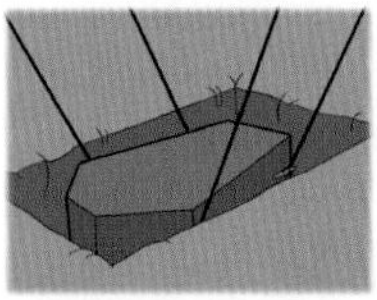

ground

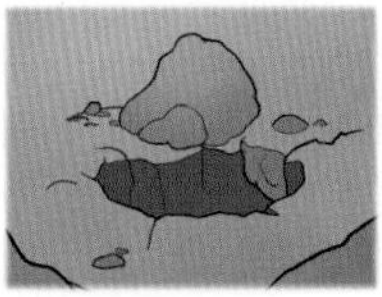

husband

When Sinbad comes out from under the ground, he meets some sailors.
'I'm Sinbad the Sailor,' he tells them.
The sailors are surprised. 'Sinbad? But Sinbad is dead,' they say.
'Well, I'm not dead now!' Sinbad says.
'And I want to meet your captain.'
The sailors take Sinbad to their ship.
'Are you Sinbad? Sinbad the Sailor?' asks the captain of the ship.
'Yes,' says Sinbad.
'Then sail with us and tell us about your adventures,' says the captain.

1 Number the sentences to tell the story.

a ☐ Sinbad meets a king and his beautiful daughter.
b [1] Sinbad goes back to sea to find more adventures.
c ☐ There's a storm and Sinbad's ship breaks.
d ☐ The sailors are surprised when they see Sinbad again.
e ☐ The king's daughter dies and the king buries Sinbad with her.
f ☐ Sinbad follows an animal and comes out of the ground.
g ☐ Sinbad marries the king's daughter.

2 Complete the story with the words.

buries | ~~daughter~~ | dies | fall in love | jewels | ill | marry

Sinbad meets the king's [1] *daughter*. They [2] ________ and they [3] ________. Sinbad is very happy, but after a year the king's daughter is very [4] ________ and she [5] ________. The king [6] ________ Sinbad with his daughter and lots of [7] ________.

3 What do they say? Write the names.

the captain | Sinbad | the king | the sailors | a friend

1 I want to go back to sea. Sinbad

2 It's time for more adventures. ____________

3 You must marry my daughter. ____________

4 Be careful! In this country they bury the husband, too. ____________

5 Sinbad? But Sinbad is dead. ____________

6 I want to meet your captain. ____________

7 Tell us about your adventures. ____________

4 What happens next? Draw.

The ship sails for many weeks. Then the ship sails into a bad storm and breaks. Sinbad lands in the sea. After many hours in the water, he arrives on a beach. Sinbad begins to explore. There are big, black rocks all around the beach and a big cave with a river in it. He finds wood from old ships and hundreds of jewels in the cave.

'More jewels!' says Sinbad and he puts some of the beautiful jewels in his bag. Soon he begins to feel hungry.

'There are lots of jewels here,' he thinks. 'But there's nothing to eat. I must look for something. But where?'

beach

cave

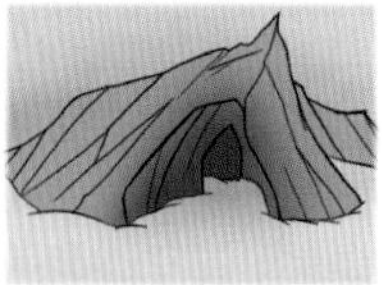

river

Sinbad takes wood from the old ships and makes a raft. He puts the raft on the river in the cave and rows for days through the dark cave. He feels more and more hungry every day. After six days he's very ill and tired. But then he sees some blue sky. He can also see two strange men.

'Welcome to the country of Serendib!' they say.

'Please give me something to eat!' cries Sinbad. The men give Sinbad lots of good things to eat.

'You're a lucky man,' say the men. 'Come with us to see our king.'

raft

row

Sinbad meets the King of Serendib. He gives the king some of the jewels from the beach. He also tells him about the most important man in Baghdad, the Caliph.

'Your Caliph is a very good and wise man,' says the king. 'Here are some presents. Please take them to him.'

Sinbad sails back to Baghdad with presents for the Caliph. He thinks about his adventure in the cave.

'This time I want to stay at home in Baghdad,' he thinks.

present

wise

When Sinbad gives the presents to the Caliph of Baghdad, the Caliph says, 'I have some beautiful carpets for this wise King of Serendib. Please take them to him.'
'Oh, no!' thinks Sinbad. 'Back to sea again!'
Sinbad sails from Baghdad again with the presents for the King of Serendib. The king is happy to see Sinbad again, but Sinbad wants to go home.
'I'm tired of adventures now,' he says.

1 Match the words with the pictures.

beach cave country ~~jewels~~ presents

raft river row

1 jewels

2 ____________

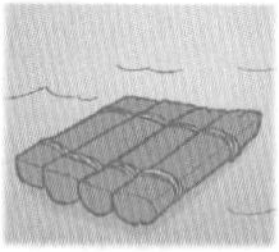

3 ____________

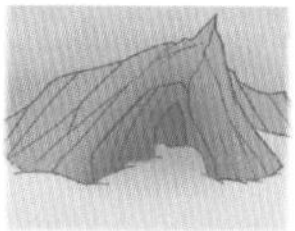

4 ____________

5 ____________

6 ____________

7 ____________

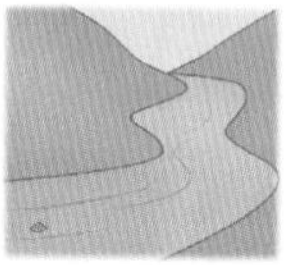

8 ____________

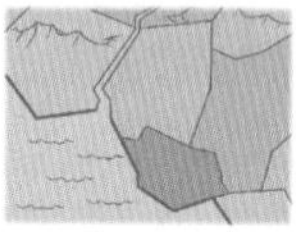

2 Complete the sentences with the words in Exercise 1.

1 Sinbad arrives on a beach and begins to explore.

2 Sinbad takes wood from old ships in the cave and makes a ____________ .

3 He puts the raft on a ____________ . Then he must ____________ through a dark ____________ .

4 After six days he arrives in the ____________ of Serendib.

5 Sinbad gives the King of Serendib some ____________ .

6 The king gives Sinbad lots of ____________ for the Caliph of Baghdad.

3 Complete the sentences.

1 After many hours in the water, Sinbad arrives ...

a ☑ on a beach. b ☐ on a ship.

2 Sinbad finds lots of jewels and ...

a ☐ wood. b ☐ trees.

3 Sinbad can't find ...

a ☐ any people. b ☐ anything to eat.

4 Sinbad makes a raft and goes ...

a ☐ through a dark cave. b ☐ on the sea.

5 Sinbad tells the king about ...

a ☐ his adventures. b ☐ the Caliph of Baghdad.

6 Sinbad sails back to Baghdad with ...

a ☐ lots of carpets. b ☐ lots of presents.

4 What happens next? Choose.

a ☐ There is a storm and the ship breaks up.

b ☐ A sea monster attacks the ship.

c ☐ Sinbad flies away with a big bird.

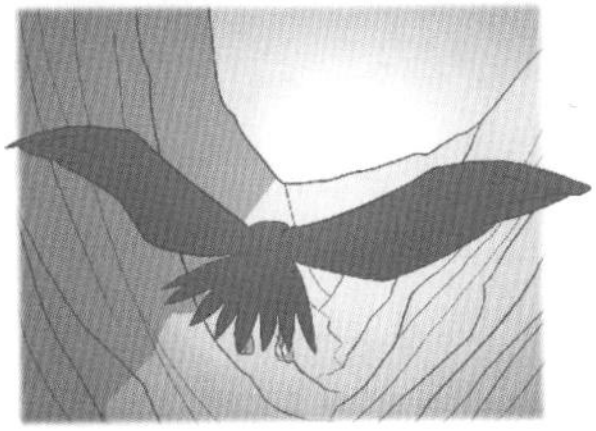

Sinbad finds a ship and sails back to Baghdad. One day a sea monster attacks the ship.
'Help!' cries Sinbad. 'Not more adventures!'
The monster is angry. It eats some of the sailors from the ship. Quickly, Sinbad gets into a little boat and rows away. The monster doesn't see Sinbad in his boat. It is looking hungrily at the sailors in the sea.
Sinbad lands on an island. He leaves his boat on the beach and goes to explore.

attack

monster

Sinbad finds a dark cave on the island. He can hear a noise.
'Someone's crying,' he thinks.
He looks into the cave and sees a young woman. In front of her, there's a monster. The monster is sleeping.
'She's the monster's prisoner,' thinks Sinbad. 'I must help her.'
That night, Sinbad waits near the cave. After some time the monster flies away to look for something to eat.
Sinbad goes into the cave.
'Come quickly,' he says to the woman.
'But who are you?' she asks.
'I'm Sinbad the Sailor,' he says. 'I can help you.'
'Thank you,' says the young woman. 'I'm Yasmin.'

cry

prisoner

Sinbad takes Yasmin to his boat on the beach.
'Can you row?' Sinbad asks her.
'Of course I can,' she says.
'Well, here's my boat. Let's row.'
Sinbad and Yasmin row all night. In the morning Sinbad sees his ship. Sinbad and Yasmin climb up to the ship.
'Sinbad!' the sailors cry. 'You're alive!'
'Of course,' says Sinbad. 'And this is my friend, Yasmin.'

Sinbad and Yasmin sail back to Baghdad. Yasmin is very excited. ‘I want to meet all your friends,’ she says.
Sinbad takes Yasmin to his house. Yasmin is surprised.
‘You’re very rich!’ she says.
‘But money isn’t the most important thing,’ says Sinbad.
‘We must spend our money wisely and help people.’
Sinbad then goes into the streets of Baghdad and he gives some of his money to the people there with no homes.
‘Thank you, Sinbad!’ they cry. ‘You’re truly a wise and good man.’

spend

street

1 Read and match.

1	One day a sea monster attacks	a	the woman.
2	Sinbad rows a little boat to	b	Baghdad.
3	Sinbad sees a young woman	c	an island.
4	Sinbad goes into the cave and helps	d	the ship.
5	Sinbad takes Yasmin back to	e	in a cave.
6	Sinbad is rich but he wants to help	f	people with no homes.

2 What do they say? Write the names.

Sinbad

Yasmin

1 *Not more adventures!* Sinbad

2 *Come quickly.* ____________

3 *Who are you?* ____________

4 *Can you row?* ____________

5 *This is my friend, Yasmin.* ____________

6 *You're very rich!* ____________

7 *We must spend our money wisely.* ____________

3 What happens next? Read and choose. Then draw.

1 Sinbad marries / doesn't marry Yasmin.

2 Sinbad stays / doesn't stay in Baghdad.

3 Sinbad is / isn't very rich.

4 Sinbad has lots more / no more adventures.

5 Sinbad goes / doesn't go to sea again.

6 Sinbad visits / doesn't visit the King of Serendib.

7 Sinbad is / isn't always lucky.

8 Sinbad finds / doesn't find lots of jewels in his garden.

9 Sinbad helps poor people / his friends .

OXFORD
UNIVERSITY PRESS

Great Clarendon Street, Oxford OX2 6DP

Oxford University Press is a department of the University of Oxford. It furthers the University's objective of excellence in research, scholarship, and education by publishing worldwide in

Oxford New York

Auckland Cape Town Dar es Salaam Hong Kong Karachi Kuala Lumpur Madrid Melbourne Mexico City Nairobi New Delhi Shanghai Taipei Toronto

With offices in

Argentina Austria Brazil Chile Czech Republic France Greece Guatemala Hungary Italy Japan Poland Portugal Singapore South Korea Switzerland Thailand Turkey Ukraine Vietnam

OXFORD and OXFORD ENGLISH are registered trade marks of Oxford University Press in the UK and in certain other countries

First published 2009
2015 2014
10

ISBN: 978 0 19 480262 8

Printed in China

This book is printed on paper from certified and well-managed sources.

ACKNOWLEDGEMENTS
Story by: Janet Hardy-Gould
Illustrated by: Dave Neale/Advocate
The Publishers would like to thank the following for their kind permission to reproduce photographs: OUP pp ii (Pyramids/John Arnold Images), ii (Athens, Istanbul/Photodisc); iStockphoto.com p ii (Baghdad/JRAustin).